Usborne Spott...

SHELLS

Graham D. Saunders

Edited by Laura Howell, Helen Gilks and
Lauris Morgan-Griffiths
Designed by Karen Tomlins and Joanne Kirkby
Digital illustrations by Verinder Bhachu
Cover designer: Joanne Kirkby
Series designer: Laura Fearn
Consultant: Dr Margaret Rostron

Acknowledgements: Shell photography 14–56 by Mike
Freeman; Cover © Getty Images/Lisa Charles Watson;
1 © Corbis; 2–3 © Michael Pole/Corbis; 8–9 © Richard
Cummins/Corbis; 12–13 © L. Clarke/Corbis; backgrounds
4–7, 10–11, 30–53, 56–64 © Digital Vision.

This edition first published in 2006 by Usborne Publishing
Ltd., Usborne House, 83-85 Saffron Hill, London, EC1N 8RT,
England. www.usborne.com

Printed in China

CONTENTS

HOW TO USE THIS BOOK

Shells are the hard, protective covering of soft-bodied animals called molluscs. When molluscs die, their empty shells are washed up on the seashore. This book helps you to identify some of the many thousands of shells that are found all over the world.

A rocky shore is a good place to find shells.

SHELL GROUPS

Shells are divided into groups called classes and smaller groups called families. Each page, headed by a class name, has a description of one or more families, and examples of shells which belong to them.

NAMING SHELLS

Each shell in this book has two names: a common name and a Latin name. Common names may vary, and not all shells have one. Latin names are used by scientists, and are the same all over the world.

WHAT'S ON A PAGE

Beside each description there is an empty circle. Tick the circle when you have seen that shell. At the end of the book is a checklist to record the date and place where you found each shell. You may see some of the rarer shells only in a shell shop or museum.

In addition to the family description, there is a small caption next to each species. This gives its common and Latin name, and typical maximum size. Coloured spots also indicate where in the world it can be found (see map, page 9).

Pilgrim's Scallop
(*Pecten jacobaeus*)
15cm

Name of species	Date seen	Where found
Piddocks	8/6	Brighton beach
Oysters	3/11	Market
Razor Shells	5/7	Shell shop
Rock Shells	10/11	Local museum

Fill in the checklist like this.

TYPES OF SHELLS

Scientists divide molluscs into different classes, based mainly on the structure of the animal and the type of shell it has. The most commonly found classes are described below.

Gastropods (e.g. limpets and whelks) have a single shell, which is usually coiled.

Chitons (also called Polyplacophora or "coat of mail" shells) have a flexible shell made up of eight overlapping plates.

Bivalves (e.g. mussels and oysters) have a shell in two halves. Each half is called a valve.

Cephalopods (e.g. ramshorns and squid) almost always have tentacles. Most have a shell, often inside, but sometimes outside their bodies.

Tusk shells (also called scaphopods) begin life as tiny bivalves. The two valves join together to form a tube which is open at both ends.

When you find a shell, decide which of the classes it belongs to and turn to the section of the book with that heading. In one of the families listed there, you should be able to see a shell similar to yours. There are many thousands of different shells found around the world, so we have shown only a selection.

PARTS OF A SHELL

The shells of different classes have very different features. Below are pictures of a gastropod and a bivalve, showing their main features. The list of useful words on page 59 will help you learn more about them. You should look for these main features when identifying a shell. Each shell family then has its own common features, which are described on the relevant pages. These will help you to narrow down your search.

Gastropod

Bivalve

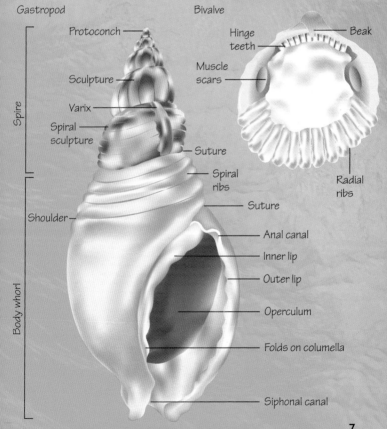

Gastropod labels: Protoconch, Sculpture, Varix, Spiral sculpture, Spire, Suture, Spiral ribs, Suture, Shoulder, Body whorl, Anal canal, Inner lip, Outer lip, Operculum, Folds on columella, Siphonal canal

Bivalve labels: Hinge teeth, Beak, Muscle scars, Radial ribs

7

For a link to a website about the parts of a shell, turn to page 62.

SHELLS OF THE WORLD

Shells which belong to the same family are generally found in similar conditions, although they may live in different parts of the world. The description of each shell family in this book tells you what type of water they prefer: tropical, warm, or cold. "Tropical" refers to the area between the two tropics (see map opposite). The coloured dots at the end of each shell's description also refer to areas of this map. Use them to find out what part of the world the shell comes from. Warm and cold seas are marked with arrows.

You would usually find a colourful shell like this in a warm or tropical sea.

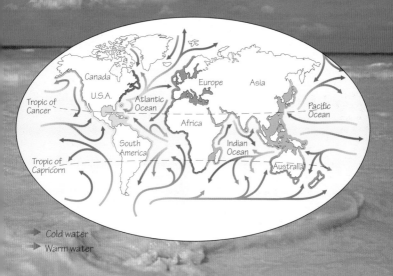

Cold water
Warm water

○ Indo-Pacific. Warm to tropical waters. A wide variety of colourful shells.

○ Australia and New Zealand. Many different families, mostly colourful.

○ Northwest America. Cool waters. Shells tend to be hardy and strong.

○ Panamic. Warm waters. Rich in colourful shells. Fewer species than in Indo-Pacific.

○ Caribbean. Warm waters. A variety of shells, many of which are large.

● Northeast America. Temperate to cold waters. Shells are strong and heavy, white or brown.

○ Northwest Europe. Cool waters, warm in places. Few colourful shells.

○ Mediterranean. Warm waters. Mostly small shells.

● West Africa. Sub-tropical to tropical waters. Many colourful, fast-growing shells.

● South Africa. Cool waters. Strong, colourful shells.

9

For a link to detailed profiles of a huge variety of shells, turn to page 62.

WHERE SHELLS ARE FOUND

Like all animals, molluscs have adapted to living in places where they have the best chance of survival; that is, where they can breed and find food and protection. Places like this are called habitats. On these pages, you can see examples of two common types of shoreline, and a list of molluscs that have adapted to living on them. The diagrams also explain in what part of these seashore habitats you can expect to find different shells. For instance, limpets and mussels will almost always be found in rocky areas.

SANDY SHORE

--- Low water line (lowest point reached by the sea at low tide)

--- High water line (highest point reached by the sea at high tide)

In the sand
Venus Shell
Cockle
Tellin
Moon Snail
Razor Shell

On rocks
Mussels
Thaid
Limpets
Top Shell

In the water
Mussels
Wentletrap
Murex
Chiton
Limpets
Scallop

LIVING TOGETHER

If you search for shells, you will probably see a number together in the same place. Shells that share a habitat often have similar shapes, even if they are not related. For instance, mud-dwelling molluscs, such as Ceriths and Spindle Shells, may have side spines or thin spires to steady themselves. Shells attached to rocks, such as Mussels and Thaids, are usually smooth and broad. Shells which live on rocks, such as Limpets and Top Shells, have heavy, bumpy shells.

ROCKY SHORE

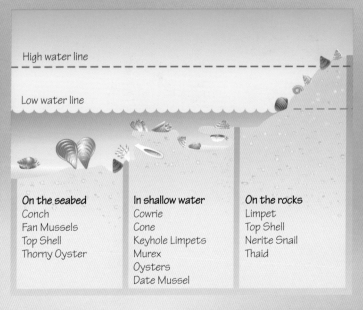

High water line

Low water line

On the seabed
Conch
Fan Mussels
Top Shell
Thorny Oyster

In shallow water
Cowrie
Cone
Keyhole Limpets
Murex
Oysters
Date Mussel

On the rocks
Limpet
Top Shell
Nerite Snail
Thaid

LOOKING FOR SHELLS

WHEN TO LOOK

The best time to look for shells is at low tide. Start at the high water level, and look among the debris washed up there. Seaweed is worth examining, as shells often cling to it.

The beach is also worth searching after a storm. Many shells may be broken, so search carefully for whole ones. Tiny microshells can often be found on sandy beaches. Sieve the sand to see what you can find.

On rocky shores, you can find shells in rock pools and tiny crevices. Try looking under small rocks, but always put them back where you found them.

Never pull a shell off a rock, or pick up any shell which still has a living creature inside. It may die if it is disturbed.

For a link to a website with advice on collecting shells, turn to page 62.

WHAT TO TAKE

If you plan to explore the beach, you may need some equipment. Here are a few of the most useful things to take:

- plastic bucket or bags to put empty shells in
- sieve for sifting sand
- notebook and pencils for recording your finds
- magnifying glass for looking at smaller shells
- small trowel for digging in the sand
- this book

TAKING NOTES

When you find a shell, make a note of its name, and the time and place where you found it. If you don't know its name, look it up in this book. You can tick off the family your shell belongs to on the checklist on pages 60-61.

KEEPING SAFE

Before you go onto a beach, make sure it is safe. Look for warning flags, and check the times of the tide so that you don't get stranded. You can get tide times in the library or from a lifeguard. NEVER look for shells on your own, and always tell an adult where you are going.

GASTROPODS

SLIPPER LIMPETS/CRUCIBLES

(Calyptraeidae). Worldwide. Flattened shells, often non-spiral. Thin shelf inside the shell. Often attached to other shells or stones. Smooth and evenly shaped.

Peruvian Hat
(*Trochatella trochiformis*)
7cm
○ ○

Shelf

Slipper Limpet
(*Crepidula fornicata*)
5cm
● ●

Hungarian Cap
(*Capulus ungaricus*)
5cm
○ ○

LIMPETS

(Patellidae). Worldwide. Flattened cone-shaped shells, evenly shaped. More pointed shells come from rough waters. Several hundred species.

Mediterranean Limpet
(*Patella caerulea*)
6cm
○ ○

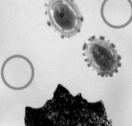

Tortoiseshell Limpet
(*Acmaea tessulata*)
2.5cm
● ●

Eye Limpet
(*Patella oculus*)
10cm
●

14

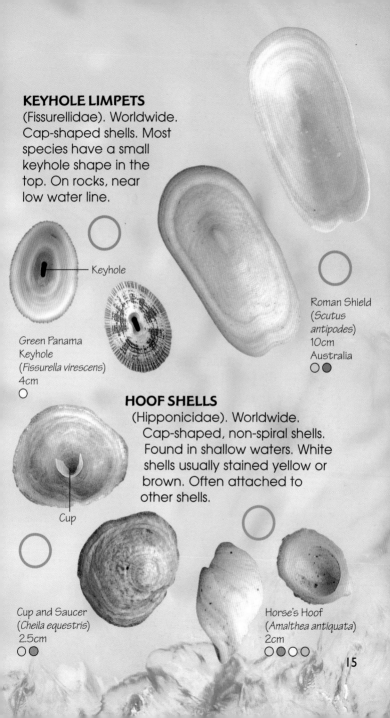

KEYHOLE LIMPETS

(Fissurellidae). Worldwide. Cap-shaped shells. Most species have a small keyhole shape in the top. On rocks, near low water line.

Keyhole

Green Panama Keyhole
(*Fissurella virescens*)
4cm
○

Roman Shield
(*Scutus antipodes*)
10cm
Australia
○ ●

HOOF SHELLS

(Hipponicidae). Worldwide. Cap-shaped, non-spiral shells. Found in shallow waters. White shells usually stained yellow or brown. Often attached to other shells.

Cup

Cup and Saucer
(*Cheila equestris*)
2.5cm
○ ●

Horse's Hoof
(*Amalthea antiquata*)
2cm
○ ○ ○ ○

GASTROPODS

SUNDIALS

(Architectonicidae).
Warm and tropical
seas. Thin shell with
large, flattened spiral.
The inside of the spiral
is lined with small,
bumpy ridges.

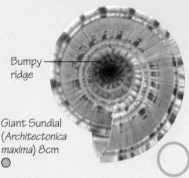

Bumpy
ridge

Giant Sundial
(*Architectonica
maxima*) 8cm
○

VIOLET SNAILS

(Janthinidae). Warm and tropical seas.
Fragile globe-like shells, with small notch
on outer lip. Violet or white.

Dwarf Purple Snail
(*Janthina exigua*) 2cm
○○○○●●

CARRIER SHELLS

(Xenophoridae). Warm
and tropical seas. Thin,
hard operculum. Empty
shells and rubble stuck
to surface of shell.

Pallid Carrier
(*Xenophora pallidula*)
10cm
○●

Mediterranean Carrier
(*Xenophora crispa*)
5cm
●

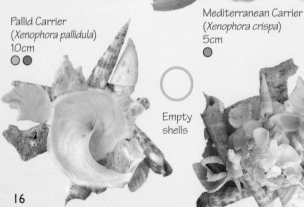

Empty
shells

ORMERS/EARSHELLS/ABALONES

(Haliotidae). All warm, cool and tropical seas except Caribbean. Flat shells with a spiral whorl and a row of breathing holes. Mother-of-pearl on inside.

Breathing holes

Black Ormer
(*Haliotis cracherodi*)
21cm
○ ●

Mother-of-pearl

Ridged
Ear Shell
(*Haliotis scalaris*)
10cm. W. Australia
○ ●

TURBAN AND STAR SHELLS

(Turbinidae). Tropical and warm seas. Medium to large shells. Found lower on the beach than Top Shells (see pages 18-19). Heavy, spiral operculum. About 500 species.

Modest Star Shell
(*Astraea modesta*)
5cm. Japan
○

Tapestry Turban
(*Turbo petholatus*)
8cm. Australia
●

17

GASTROPODS

TOP SHELLS
(Trochidae). Worldwide.
Shells from deep water
are pointed and thin with
fine surface sculpture.
Shells from shallow
water are heavy and
rounded. Round, hard
operculum. Inside the
shell is mother-of-pearl.

Snake Skin Top Shell
(*Tegula pellisserpentis*)
3cm

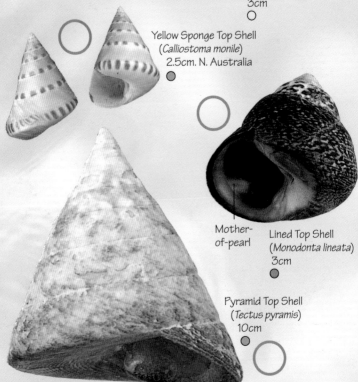

Yellow Sponge Top Shell
(*Calliostoma monile*)
2.5cm. N. Australia

Mother-
of-pearl

Lined Top Shell
(*Monodonta lineata*)
3cm

Pyramid Top Shell
(*Tectus pyramis*)
10cm

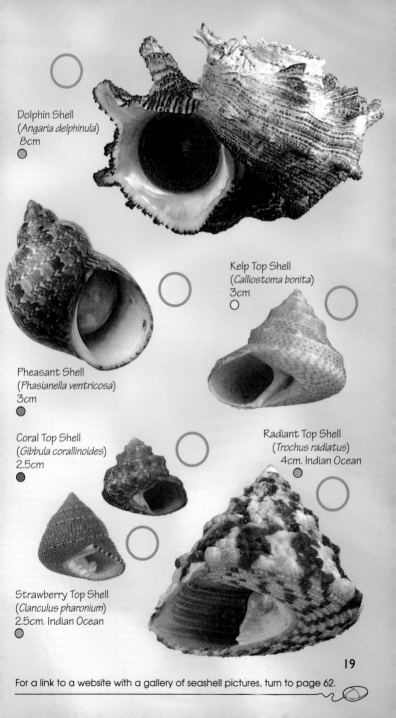

Dolphin Shell
(*Angaria delphinula*)
8cm

Pheasant Shell
(*Phasianella ventricosa*)
3cm

Kelp Top Shell
(*Calliostoma bonita*)
3cm

Coral Top Shell
(*Gibbula corallinoides*)
2.5cm

Radiant Top Shell
(*Trochus radiatus*)
4cm. Indian Ocean

Strawberry Top Shell
(*Clanculus pharonium*)
2.5cm. Indian Ocean

19

For a link to a website with a gallery of seashell pictures, turn to page 62.

GASTROPODS

PERIWINKLES/WINKLES

(Littorinidae). Worldwide.
Cold-water shells are
rounded and heavy.
Tropical shells are thinner
with high spires.

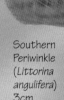

Southern
Periwinkle
(*Littorina
angulifera*)
3cm
○

Flat Periwinkle
(*Littorina
obtusata*)
1.5cm
○○

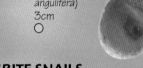

NERITE SNAILS

(Neritidae). Tropical and
warm seas. Strong and
often colourful. Broad
body whorl. Hook on
operculum.

Chameleon Nerite
(*Nerita chameleon*)
3cm. Australia
○

Bleeding Tooth
(*Nerita peloronta*)
4cm
○

TURRETS/SCREW SHELLS

(Turritellidae). Warm and
tropical seas. Long, thin spiral
shells, live buried in sand or
mud below water line.

Round
opening

European Screw Shell
(*Turritella communis*)
4cm
○○ ○

HORN SHELLS/NEEDLE WHELKS

(Cerithidae). Worldwide, but more common in tropical seas. Identified by siphonal canal which twists back.

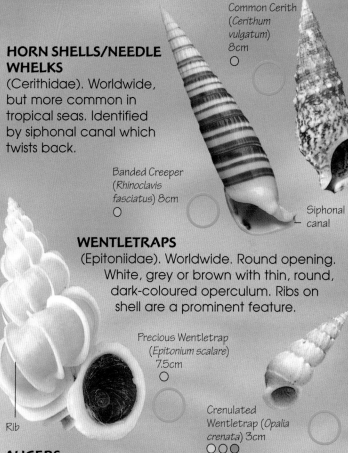

Common Cerith (*Cerithum vulgatum*) 8cm
○

Banded Creeper (*Rhinoclavis fasciatus*) 8cm
○

Siphonal canal

WENTLETRAPS

(Epitoniidae). Worldwide. Round opening. White, grey or brown with thin, round, dark-coloured operculum. Ribs on shell are a prominent feature.

Precious Wentletrap (*Epitonium scalare*) 7.5cm
○

Rib

Crenulated Wentletrap (*Opalia crenata*) 3cm
○○○

AUGERS

(Terebridae). Tropical and warm seas. Long, thin spire. Augers distinguished from Turret and Horn shells by shape of siphonal canal.

Lance Auger (*Terebra lanceata*) 8cm
W. Pacific
○

GASTROPODS

WORM SHELLS
(Vermetidae). Warm and tropical seas. Young shells shaped like pointed turrets, but then grow unevenly into worm-like shapes. About 50 species.

Knorr's Worm
(*Vermicularia knorri*)
10cm

TURRIDS
(Turridae). Worldwide. Small shells with notch at the suture. Small opening. Hard operculum. More than 1,200 species. Up to 15cm.

Notch

Rose Turrid (*Clavus rosalina*) 4cm

TUN SHELLS
(Tonnidae). Tropical and warm seas. Large, thin shells with spiral ridges. White, yellow or brown in colour. Often damaged when found on beaches.

Banded Tun
(*Tonna sulcosa*)
12cm

Partridge Tun
(*Tonna perdix*)
20cm

FIG SHELLS

(Ficidae). Tropical seas, except
W. Africa. Long siphonal canal.
Finely sculptured with
criss-crossed surface.
Fewer than 15 species.

Spotted Fig (*Ficus
ficoides*) 10cm

MOON SNAILS/NECKLACE SHELLS

(Naticidae). Worldwide. Strong, shiny
shells which can be thick, rounded
or flattened. Small spire with few
whorls. Large opening. Operculum
usually semicircular.

Baby
Ear (*Sinum
perspectivum*)
4cm

Colourful Atlantic Moon Snail
(*Naticarius canrena*)
4cm

Lightning Moon Shell
(*Natica fulminia*) 3cm

Shark Eye
(*Polinices duplicatus*)
8cm

23

GASTROPODS

TULIP SHELLS

(Fasciolariidae). Tropical and warm seas. Smooth columella with fine tooth-like marks on outer lip. Living animal is usually bright red. Smooth shell with thick and hairy or smooth and thin periostracum.

Needle Tooth
(*Opeatostoma pseudodon*)
4.5cm

Hunter's Tulip
(*Fasciolaria hunteria*)
10cm

Fischer's Tulip
(*Fasciolaria buxea*) 10cm

Knobbly Latirus
(*Latirus polygonus*)
8cm

Columella ———

Distaff Spindle
(*Fusinus colus*)
20cm

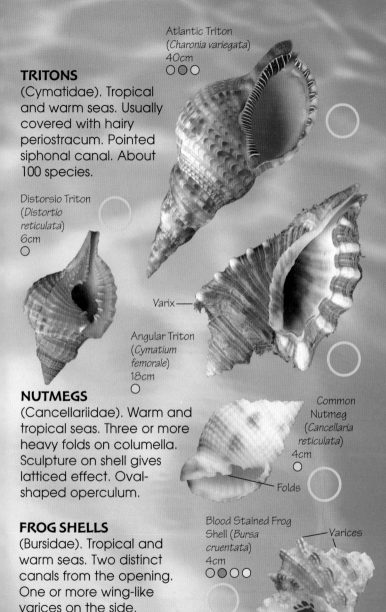

TRITONS

(Cymatidae). Tropical and warm seas. Usually covered with hairy periostracum. Pointed siphonal canal. About 100 species.

Atlantic Triton
(*Charonia variegata*)
40cm
○○○

Distorsio Triton
(*Distortio reticulata*)
6cm
○

Varix —

Angular Triton
(*Cymatium femorale*)
18cm
○

NUTMEGS

(Cancellariidae). Warm and tropical seas. Three or more heavy folds on columella. Sculpture on shell gives latticed effect. Oval-shaped operculum.

Common Nutmeg
(*Cancellaria reticulata*)
4cm
○

— Folds

FROG SHELLS

(Bursidae). Tropical and warm seas. Two distinct canals from the opening. One or more wing-like varices on the side.

Blood Stained Frog Shell (*Bursa cruentata*)
4cm
○○○○

— Varices

Canals —

25

GASTROPODS

MUREX SHELLS

(Muricidae). Worldwide, but most are tropical. Long or short siphonal canal. Shells have spines, knobs or horns like wings. Operculum hard and dark brown. Some live on rocks, but more delicate shells are found on mud. Several hundred species.

Callidan Murex
(*Muricanthus callidinus*)
10cm
O

Venus Comb
(*Murex pecten*)
15cm
O

Dye Murex
(*Bolinus brandaris*)
10cm
O O

Ramose Murex
(*Chicoreus ramosus*)
30cm
O

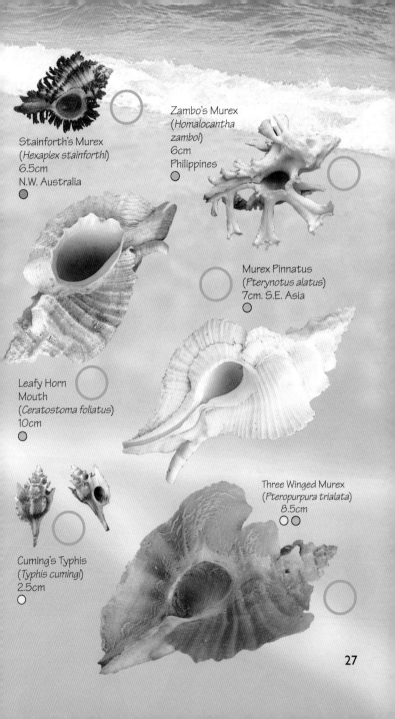

Stainforth's Murex
(*Hexaplex stainforthi*)
6.5cm
N.W. Australia

Zambo's Murex
(*Homalocantha
zamboi*)
6cm
Philippines

Murex Pinnatus
(*Pterynotus alatus*)
7cm. S.E. Asia

Leafy Horn
Mouth
(*Ceratostoma foliatus*)
10cm

Three Winged Murex
(*Pteropurpura trialata*)
8.5cm

Cuming's Typhis
(*Typhis cumingi*)
2.5cm

GASTROPODS

ROCK SHELLS/DYE SHELLS

(Thaididae). Worldwide. Solid, low-spired shells with a large body whorl. Wide opening. Operculum red/brown, thin and hard. Usually small knobs around the shell. Found on rocks between high and low water.

Rock Shell
(*Thais haemostoma*)
8cm
○ ○ ○

Garland Thaid
(*Nassa serta*)
7cm
E. Australia
○

Cart Rut Shell
(*Neothais scalaris*)
10cm. New Zealand
○

Red Mouth Drupe (*Drupa rubusidaea*)
5.5cm
○

Wide Mouth Rock Shell
(*Purpura patula*)
10cm
○

CORAL SNAILS

(Coralliophilidae).
Warm and tropical
seas. Round, often
spiny, with many small
spiral ridges. Mostly
white. Often live
near coral.

Violet Coral Snail
(*Coralliophila
neritoidea*)
6cm. Japan

Mawa's Pagoda
(*Latiaxis mawae*)
7cm. Japan

Meyendorff's
Coral Snail
(*Coralliophilia
meyendorffi*)
4cm

FALSE TRITONS

(Colubrariidae). Tropical
seas. Distinguished from
real Tritons (see page 25)
by thickening of the shell
near the opening. Under
rocks in shallow water.

False Triton
(*Colubraria reticulata*)
3.5cm

Giant False
Triton (*Colubraria
maculosa*)
10cm. W. Pacific

29

For a link to an interactive guide to shell identification, turn to page 62.

GASTROPODS

DOG WHELKS

(Nassariidae). Worldwide. Most have latticed sculpture. Short, slightly twisted siphonal canal. Lip thicker than the rest of the shell.

Siphonal canal —

Wolff's Dog Whelk (*Nassarius wolffi*) 5cm

Thickened lip

Unicolour Dog Whelk (*Zeuxis dorsatus*) 3cm. W. Australia

Moroccan Bullia (*Bullia miran*) 3.5cm

WHELKS

(Buccinidae). Worldwide. Similar to Dog Whelks, but usually larger. In mature shells, lip is thinner than rest of the shell. Thick periostracum.

No thickening of lip

New England Neptune (*Neptunea decemcostata*) 12cm

Channelled Babylon (*Babylonia canaliculata*) 7cm. N. Indian Ocean

Whelk (*Buccinum undatum*) 15cm

Japanese Bonnet
(*Phalium bisulcatum*)
7cm
○

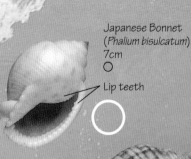

Lip teeth

HELMET SHELLS

(Cassidae). Tropical seas.
Large, heavy shells often
with wide, strong lips. Teeth
on one or both lips. Siphonal
canal twists and turns back.
About 80 species.

Scotch Bonnet
(*Phalium granulatum*)
7cm
○ ● ○

Bull Mouth
(*Cypraecassis rufa*)
18cm
○

King Helmet
(*Cassis tuberosa*)
23cm
○ ●

Canal twists back

GASTROPODS

STROMBS/CONCHES
(Strombidae). Tropical
and warm seas. Young
shells can be mistaken
for Cone Shells (see
page 36) before they
have developed their
strong, broad outer lip.
Notch at the side, known
as "stromboid notch".

Fighting Conch
(*Strombus pugilus*)
9cm
○

Stromboid
notch

Lister's Conch
(*Strombus listeri*)
15cm
S.E. Asia
○

Powis' Tibia
(*Tibia powisi*)
5cm
Pacific
○

Dwarf Tibia
(*Varicospira
cancellata*)
3cm
Pacific
○

Spider Stromb
(*Lambis lambis*)
20cm
○

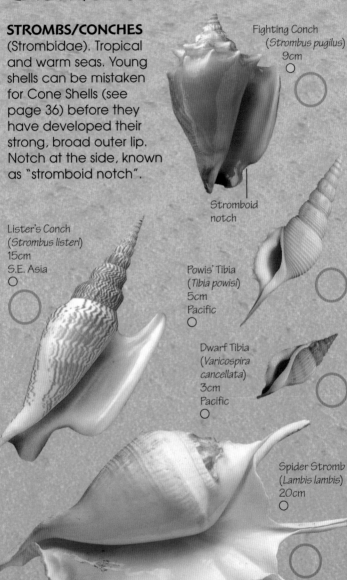

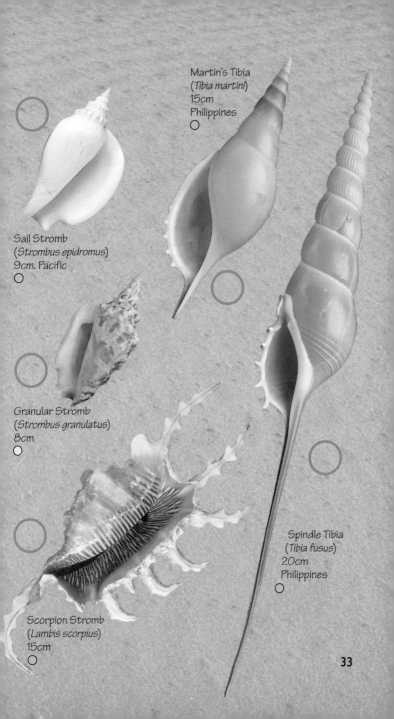

Martin's Tibia
(*Tibia martini*)
15cm
Philippines
○

Sail Stromb
(*Strombus epidromus*)
9cm. Pacific
○

Granular Stromb
(*Strombus granulatus*)
8cm
○

Scorpion Stromb
(*Lambis scorpius*)
15cm
○

Spindle Tibia
(*Tibia fusus*)
20cm
Philippines
○

GASTROPODS

OSTRICH FOOT SHELLS

(Struthiolaridae).
New Zealand, Australia
and Indian Ocean.
Fragile, brown shells with
thickened lip. Heavy
white thickening
around opening.

Ostrich Foot
(*Struthiolaria
papulosa*)
9cm
New Zealand

PELICAN FOOT/DUCK FOOT SHELLS

(Aporrhaidae). N. Atlantic,
Mediterranean, W. Africa. Wide
lip, usually with straight spines.
Five living species.

West African Bird Foot
(*Aporrhais
senegalensis*)
3cm

Pelican's Foot
(*Aporrhais pespelicani*)
6cm

Vase Shell
(*Vasum muricatum*)
13cm

VASE SHELLS

(Vasidae). Tropical seas. Heavy
shells, usually white with dark
markings on their blunt spines.
Hairy periostracum.

Snipe head
(*Tudicula inermis*)
8cm
N.W. Australia

34

CROWN CONCHES

(Melongenidae).
Tropical seas.
Short-spired,
heavy shell with
long siphonal
canal. Periostracum
usually thick and
quite rubbery. Living
animal feeds on
other molluscs.

Lightning Whelk
(*Busycon contrarium*)
40cm. E. Africa

Siphonal
canal

Crown Conch
(*Melongena corona*)
10cm

Fig Whelk
(*Busycon spiratum*)
13cm

35

GASTROPODS

HARP SHELLS
(Harpidae). Tropical seas. Attractive shells with obvious varices which show growth stages. About 12 species.

Rose Harp
(*Harpa doris*)
7.5cm

Articulated Harp
(*Harpa articularis*) 10cm

CONE SHELLS
(Conidae). Tropical seas. Uniform cone or cylinder-type shells with long, narrow opening. Most of the living animals have a poisonous sting

Court Cone
(*Conus aulicus*)
7cm

Prince Cone
(*Conus princeps*)
7cm

Fig Cone
(*Conus figulinus*)
8cm

MITRES

(Mitridae). Tropical and warm seas. Slim, long and colourful. Folds on columella. Thin periostracum. Most have spiral ridges.

Thread Mitre
(*Cancilla filaris*)
3cm
○

Cone Mitre
(*Imbricaria conularis*)
2.5cm
○

Little Fox
(*Vexillum vulpecula*)
7cm
W. Pacific
○

Diadem Mitre
(*Mitra puncticulata*)
6cm
○

Dactylus Mitre
(*Pterygia dactylus*)
5cm
○

GASTROPODS

MARGIN SHELLS

(Marginellidae). Warm and tropical seas. Spire short or covered by body whorl. Usually 3-5 folds on columella. Thick outer lip. No periostracum. Smooth, shiny shells.

Loup Margin
(*Persicula phyrgia*)
0.5cm

Orange Margin
(*Prunum oblonga*)
2.5cm

Philippine Margin
(*Volvarina philippinarium*)
1.5cm
W. Pacific

Desjardin's Margin
(*Marginella desjardini*)
7cm

Thick outer lip

Folds on columella

Striper Margin
(*Perisicula cingula*)
2cm

Pink Margin
(*Marginella irrorata*)
3cm

Folds on columella

38

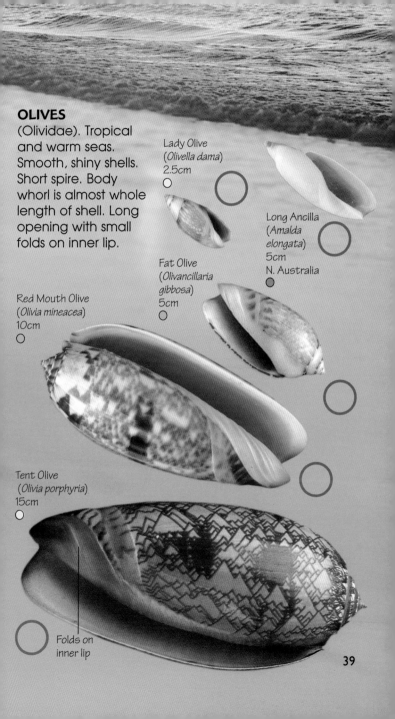

OLIVES

(Olividae). Tropical and warm seas. Smooth, shiny shells. Short spire. Body whorl is almost whole length of shell. Long opening with small folds on inner lip.

Lady Olive
(*Olivella dama*)
2.5cm
○

Long Ancilla
(*Amalda elongata*)
5cm
N. Australia
●

Fat Olive
(*Olivancillaria gibbosa*)
5cm
○

Red Mouth Olive
(*Olivia mineacea*)
10cm
○

Tent Olive
(*Olivia porphyria*)
15cm
○

Folds on inner lip

39

GASTROPODS

VOLUTES

(Volutidae). Temperate, warm and tropical seas, especially in Australia. Shells mostly thick, shiny, heavy and colourful. Usually large protoconch, which is often smooth and rounded.

Hallia
(*Ampulla priamus*)
9cm

Hebrew Volute
(*Voluta ebraea*)
15cm

Junonia Volute
(*Scaphella junonia*)
14cm

Damon's Volute
(*Amoria damoni*)
15cm. Australia

Baler Shell
(*Melo amphorus*)
25cm
W. Pacific

40

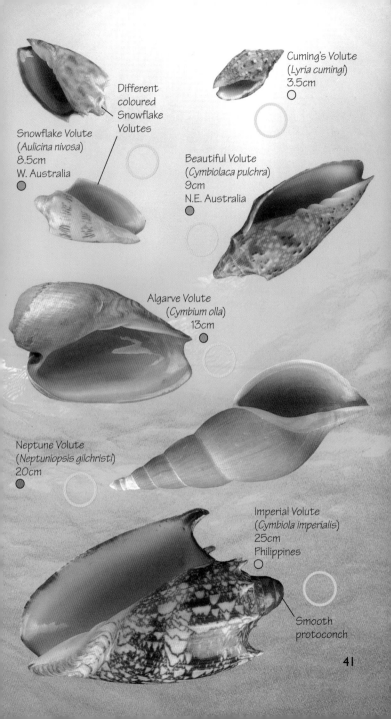

Cuming's Volute
(*Lyria cumingi*)
3.5cm
○

Different
coloured
Snowflake
Volutes

Snowflake Volute
(*Aulicina nivosa*)
8.5cm
W. Australia
●

Beautiful Volute
(*Cymbiolaca pulchra*)
9cm
N.E. Australia
●

Algarve Volute
(*Cymbium olla*)
13cm
●

Neptune Volute
(*Neptuniopsis gilchristi*)
20cm
●

Imperial Volute
(*Cymbiola imperialis*)
25cm
Philippines
○

Smooth
protoconch

GASTROPODS

COWRIES

(Cypraeidae). Tropical and warm seas. Body whorl forms the whole shell. Shiny, smooth shells with a row of "teeth" on both lips. About 180 species.

Little Deer Cowrie (*Cypraea cervinetta*)
9cm

Teeth on both lips

Sieve Cowrie (*Cypraea cribraria*)
3.5cm

Atlantic Cowrie (*Cypraea spurca*)
3cm

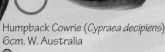

Humpback Cowrie (*Cypraea decipiens*)
6cm. W. Australia

BUTTON SHELLS

(Eratoidae). Tropical and warm seas. Small shells, similar to Cowries but with grooves across the back of the shell. Many are microshells.

Radiant Button Shell (*Trivia radians*)
2cm

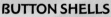

European Cowrie (*Trivia monacha*)
1.5cm

42

For a link to a website with an illustrated guide to shells, turn to page 62.

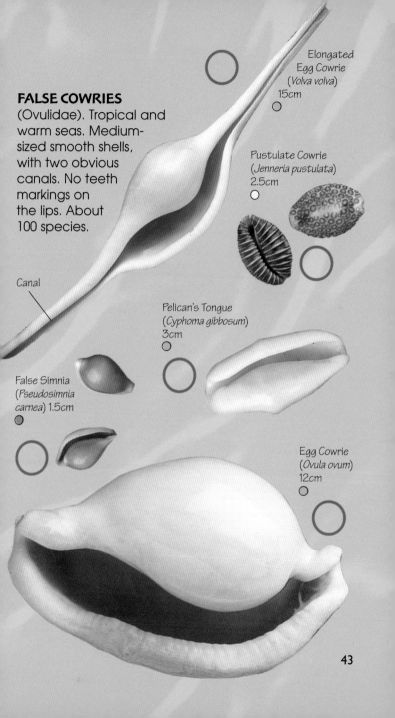

FALSE COWRIES
(Ovulidae). Tropical and warm seas. Medium-sized smooth shells, with two obvious canals. No teeth markings on the lips. About 100 species.

Elongated Egg Cowrie (*Volva volva*) 15cm

Pustulate Cowrie (*Jenneria pustulata*) 2.5cm

Canal

Pelican's Tongue (*Cyphoma gibbosum*) 3cm

False Simnia (*Pseudosimnia carnea*) 1.5cm

Egg Cowrie (*Ovula ovum*) 12cm

GASTROPODS

DOVE SHELLS
(Pyrenidae). Warm
and tropical seas.
Strong, small, colourful
shells. Often in large
numbers in seaweed.
Usually covered in lime
or weed when alive.

Rustic Dove Shell
(*Pyrene rustica*)
2.5cm
○ ○

Humped Strombina
(*Strombina
dorsata*)
3cm
○

BUBBLE SHELLS
(Opisthobranchia). Tropical
and warm seas. Thin, fragile
shells. Thin outer lip. Sunken
spire. Found in sand and mud.

White Banded Bubble
(*Hydatina albocincta*)
6cm
○

Pacific Bubble
(*Bulla ampulla*)
6cm
○

Canoe Shell
(*Scaphander lignarius*)
7cm
○ ○

Sunken
spire

BIVALVES

ARK SHELLS

(Arcidae). Worldwide. Straight
hinge with many teeth fitting
closely together. Equal valves.

Ponderous Ark
(*Noetia ponderosa*)
6cm

Exterior

Turkey Wing
(*Arca zebra*)
9cm

Hinge teeth

Interior

NUT SHELLS

(Nuculidae). Worldwide. Small,
strong shells with pearly interior.
Many tiny hinge teeth.
Equal valves.

Nut Shell
(*Nucula nucleus*)
1.2cm

DOG COCKLES/BITTER SWEETS

(Glycymerididae). Worldwide.
Round, heavy shells with
saw-like edges. Two groups
of hinge teeth parallel
to edge of shell.

Bitter Sweet
(*Petunculus formosus*)
9cm

BIVALVES

MUSSELS

(Mytilidae). Worldwide.
Blue or brown. Mollusc
lives attached to rocks
by threads. Valves are
equal size and do not
have teeth. Edible.
Very common.

Yellow Mussel
(*Brachidontes
citrinus*)
5cm

Date Mussel
(*Lithophaga
lithophaga*)
7cm

Blue mussel
(Mytilus edulis)
12cm

Horse Mussel
(*Modiolus modiolus*)
22cm

CARDITAS

(Carditidae). Worldwide. Small, often
elongated shells with distinct ribs. Equal
valves. One major hinge tooth. Under
stones in shallow water.

European Cardita
(*Cardita calyculata*)
2.5cm

Radiant Cardita
(*Cardita radians*) 4.5cm

46

For a link to a site with shell activities, games and jokes, turn to page 62.

COCKLES

(Cardidae). Worldwide. Heart-shaped shell. Most have strong ribs with saw-like edges. Two central teeth on hinge, and usually one or two teeth on each side of hinge.

Egg Cockle
(*Laevicardium laevigatum*)
4cm

Saw-like edge ——

China Cockle
(*Trachycardium egmontianum*)
4cm

GIANT CLAMS

(Tridacnidae). Tropical areas of Indo-Pacific. Large, thick, heavy shells. Gap near the hinge through which the living mollusc anchors itself. Six species.

Long Giant Clam
(*Tridacna elongata*)
32cm

—— Gap

Fluted Giant Clam
(*Tridacna squamosa*)
40cm

BIVALVES

OYSTERS
(Ostreidae). Worldwide.
Large, heavy shells,
outer edges flaky and
fragile. One valve smaller
than the other.

European
Oyster
attached to
whelk shell

Cock's Comb
(*Lopha cristigalli*)
9cm
○

European
Oyster
(*Ostrea edulis*)
12cm
●●

SADDLE OYSTERS
(Anomidae). Worldwide. Hole
in lower valve through which living
mollusc attaches itself to rocks.

— Hole

Saddle Oyster
(*Anomia
ephippium*)
7cm
●●●

FLAT OYSTERS

(Isognominidae). Tropical parts of Atlantic and Pacific. Flat shells with a long, straight row of hinge teeth.

Flat Oyster
(*Isognomon isognomon*)
12cm
○○○◒

Pearl Oyster
(*Pinctada margaritifera*)
18cm
○

PEARL OYSTERS

(Pteriidae). Tropical and warm seas. Outside is scaly, inside is mother-of-pearl. Wing-like extensions on hinge.

Mother-of-pearl

Blue pearly interior

HAMMER OYSTERS

(Malleidae). Tropical Indo-Pacific. Wide base and narrow body. Blue pearly interior near the hinge.

White Hammer Oyster
(*Malleus albus*) 20cm
○

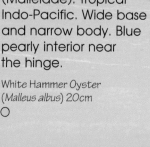

BIVALVES

FILE SHELLS

(Limidae). Worldwide. White shell with distinct ribs. Has small "ears" and a beak which extends past the hinge.

Iredale's Giant File
(*Lima persquamifer*)
10cm
○

Eastern Lion's Paw
(*Lyropecten corallinoides*)
6cm
●

SCALLOPS

(Pectinidae). Tropical and warm seas. Often colourful. Has an "ear" on either side of beak - one usually larger than the other. Several hundred species.

"Ear"

Beak

Pilgrim's Scallop
(*Pecten jacobaeus*)
15cm
○ ●

Australian Scallop
(*Chlamys australis*)
9cm
Australia
● ○

Calico Scallop
(*Aequipecten gibbus*)
50cm
● ○

THORNY OYSTERS

(Spondylidae).
Tropical and warm
seas. Often has
long or short spines.

Red Thorny Oyster
(*Spondylus coccineus*)
8cm. Philippines
○

Oyster
attached
to coral

JEWEL BOXES

(Chamidae). Tropical
seas. Beak usually
strongly curved. Shape
varies. Usually covered in
seaweed or dead coral.

Leaf Chama
(*Chama lazarus*) 15cm
○

VENUS CLAMS

(Veneriidae) Worldwide.
Strong, heavy shells.
Small but long hinge
teeth. Muscle scars
on inside of shell.

Tent Venus
(*Lioconcha castrenis*)
4.5cm
○

Lamellate Venus
(*Antigonia lamellaris*)
4.5cm
W. Pacific
○

Kellet's Venus
(*Chione kelletia*)
4cm
○

51

For a link to a website about different types of molluscs, turn to page 62.

BIVALVES

WEDGE SHELLS
(Donacidae).
Worldwide. Small,
shiny, wedge-shaped
shell with saw-like
edge. Both valves
same size.

Great False
Coquina (*Iphigenia
brasiliensis*) 7cm
○

Panama Coquina
(*Donax panamensis*)
4cm
○

TELLINS
(Tellinidae). Worldwide. Flat, thin,
usually delicate shell. Stripes of colour
on shell. Valves often unequal.

Flat Tellin
(*Tellina
planata*)
6cm
○○

Sunrise Shell
(*Tellina radiata*)
6cm
○

Stanger's Sanguin
(*Gari stangeri*)
6cm
New Zealand
○

SUNSET SHELLS

(Psammobiidae).
Worldwide. Thin, flat shells.
Similar to Tellins, but more
symmetrical. Equal valves
which have a gap at
each end when closed.

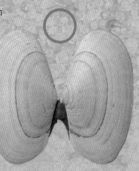

TROUGH SHELLS

(Mactridae). Worldwide. Shells
either heavy and white or fragile
and thin. Pale blue or yellow.
Triangular dent in hinge.

Australian Surf Clam
(*Mactra australis*)
5cm
●

Violet Surf Clam
(*Mactra violacea*)
8cm
○

LUCINES

(Lucinidae). Worldwide.
Thin, round shells. Most
are white. Small but
distinct beak.

Beak

Buttercup
Lucine
(*Anodonta
alba*) 5cm
○ ●

Orb Lucine
(*Codakia
orbicularis*)
8cm
○

Beak

Beak

53

BIVALVES

RAZOR SHELLS

(Solenidae). Worldwide.
Long, oblong shells. Valves
do not close at either end.
Small hinge at corner of one
end only.

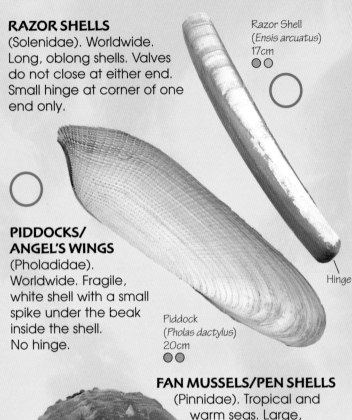

Razor Shell
(*Ensis arcuatus*)
17cm

PIDDOCKS/
ANGEL'S WINGS

(Pholadidae).
Worldwide. Fragile,
white shell with a small
spike under the beak
inside the shell.
No hinge.

Hinge

Piddock
(*Pholas dactylus*)
20cm

FAN MUSSELS/PEN SHELLS

(Pinnidae). Tropical and
warm seas. Large,
fan-shaped shell.
No teeth on hinge.

Fan Mussel
(*Pinna rudis*)
45cm

CHITONS AND TUSK SHELLS

CHITONS
(Polyplacophora).
Worldwide. All made up
of eight plates which
overlap and are joined
by a leathery girdle.
Shell is flexible and
smooth or spiny.
Difficult to preserve.

Spiny Chiton
(*Acanthopleura spinosa*)
15cm. N. Australia

Lined Chiton
(*Tonicella lineata*)
4cm

Leathery
girdle

TUSK SHELLS
(Scaphopoda).
Worldwide. Long shells,
open at both ends. Buried
in mud in deep water. Often
washed up on beaches after
storms. Over 300 species.

Elephant Tooth
(*Dentalium
elephantium*)
35cm

Rosy Tooth
(*Dentalium
rubescens*)
9cm

55

For a link to a site with videos of cuttlefish and squid, turn to page 62.

CEPHALOPODS

CEPHALOPODS

(Cephalopoda).
Worldwide. This class of
molluscs includes squid,
octopus, cuttlefish, and
nautilus. More than 50
species, but not all have
shells. Almost all living
animals have tentacles.

Chambered Nautilus
(*Nautilus pompilius*)
20cm

Paper Nautilus
(*Argonauta argo*)
20cm

Ramshorn
(*Spirula spirula*)
3.5cm
Worldwide

Cuttlefish
(*Sepia officinalis*)
25cm
Worldwide

Rough,
transparent
edges

Brown Paper Nautilus
(*Argonauta hians*)
75cm. Worldwide

LOOKING AT MOLLUSCS

All molluscs have a soft body and no skeleton. The body is surrounded by a thin layer called the mantle, from which the shell is formed. A mollusc can withdraw into its shell to hide from danger. The body is usually divided into a head, a muscular "foot", and a body mass. This contains the major organs, such as the heart and stomach.

GASTROPODS

Most gastropods have coiled shells. A hard pad called an operculum seals the shell's opening when the animal is inside. On the animal's head is a pair of tentacles, which carries the sense organs. There is also a tube called a siphon, which takes clean water over the gills. This supplies the animal with oxygen.

BIVALVES

Bivalves have two shells, called valves, which are hinged. The shells are kept closed by a pair of strong muscles. Some bivalves live attached to rocks, others burrow in sand, mud or rock. They dig and move around using their muscular foot.

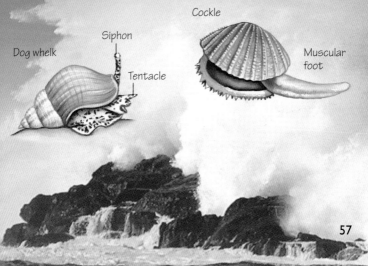

Cockle

Dog whelk

Siphon

Tentacle

Muscular foot

LIFE CYCLE OF A MOLLUSC

Molluscs produce their young in different ways. Some lay eggs which hatch into tiny shelled "crawlers", while some give birth to live "crawlers". Others lay eggs which hatch into "veligers". A veliger is free-swimming and has the beginning of a shell.

Thousands of tiny veligers hatch from hundreds of egg capsules. Most of these veligers are eaten by fish and other animals, and others never find a suitable habitat (a safe place to feed and grow). This means that only a few survive to become adults.

Unlike veligers, crawlers are born into their own natural habitat. This means that fewer need to be laid to make sure that some survive.

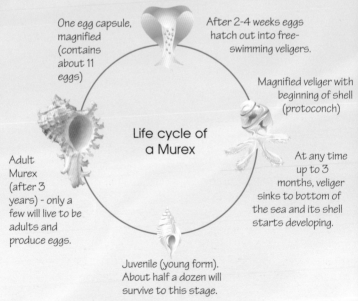

One egg capsule, magnified (contains about 11 eggs)

After 2-4 weeks eggs hatch out into free-swimming veligers.

Magnified veliger with beginning of shell (protoconch)

Life cycle of a Murex

At any time up to 3 months, veliger sinks to bottom of the sea and its shell starts developing.

Adult Murex (after 3 years) - only a few will live to be adults and produce eggs.

Juvenile (young form). About half a dozen will survive to this stage.

For a link to a site with movies of endangered molluscs, turn to page 62.

USEFUL WORDS

aperture – opening in a gastropod shell.

beak – earliest formed part of a bivalve shell.

bivalve – mollusc with two shells, called valves, hinged together.

body whorl – last and largest coil of a gastropod shell.

columella – central pillar at the opening of a gastropod shell.

crawlers – young molluscs that have a shell when they hatch.

ear – small flat pieces on a bivalve on either side of the hinge.

gastropod – mollusc with a single shell which is usually coiled.

hinge teeth – interlocking devices which keep the two halves of a bivalve together.

lip – outer edge of a gastropod shell opening.

mantle – fold of "skin" covering a mollusc's body.

microshells – very small species of shells.

muscle scars – marks on the inside of an empty bivalve shell. These show where the muscles which pulled the valves together were attached.

operculum – hard material on a gastropod's foot that seals the shell when the animal is inside.

periostracum – thin layer of hard material that protects the shell.

protoconch – first formed part of a gastropod shell.

shoulder – lump or ridge on the side of a body whorl.

siphonal canal – channel at the bottom of a gastropod shell opening.

spire – part of a gastropod shell above the body whorl.

suture – the place where two whorls join.

valve – one of a bivalve's pair of shells.

varices – thickened parts of a shell, formed during a pause in its growth. A single one is called a varix.

veliger – free-swimming, shell-less young of some mollusc species.

whorl – one complete coil of a gastropod shell.

CHECKLIST

The shell families in this checklist are arranged in alphabetical order. When you find a shell belonging to any of these families, fill in the date and the place where you saw it.

You can mark off families that are not found on local shores if you see them in museums or shell shops. Mark off individual species in the tick circles next to them.

Name of species	Date seen	Where spotted	Name of species	Date seen	Where spotted
Ark Shells			False Cowries		
Augers			False Tritons		
Bitter Sweets			Fan Mussels		
Bubble Shells			Fig Shells		
Button Shells			File Shells		
Carditas			Flat Oysters		
Carrier Shells			Frog Shells		
Cephalopods			Giant Clams		
Chitons			Hammer Oysters		
Cockles			Harp Shells		
Cone Shells			Helmet Shells		
Coral Snails			Hoof Shells		
Cowries			Horn Shells		
Crown Conches			Jewel Boxes		
Dog Cockles			Keyhole Limpets		
Dog Whelks			Limpets		
Dove Shells			Lucines		

Name of species	Date seen	Where spotted	Name of species	Date seen	Where spotted
Margin Shells			Sundials		
Mitres			Sunset Shells		
Moon Snails			Surf Clams		
Murex Shells			Tellins		
Mussels			Thorny Oysters		
Nerite Snails			Top Shells		
Nut Shells			Tritons		
Nutmegs			Trough Shells		
Olives			Tulip Shells		
Ormers/Abalones			Tun Shells		
Ostrich Foot Shells			Turban Shells		
Pearl Oysters			Turrets		
Pelican Foot Shells			Turrids		
Periwinkles			Tusk Shells		
Piddocks			Vase Shells		
Oysters			Venus Clams		
Razor Shells			Violet Shells		
Rock Shells			Volutes		
Saddle Oysters			Wedge Shells		
Scallops			Wentletraps		
Slipper Limpets			Whelks		
Strombs			Worm Shells		

INTERNET LINKS

If you have access to the Internet, you can visit these websites to find out more about shells. For links to these sites, go to the Usborne Quicklinks Website at **www.usborne-quicklinks.com** and enter the keywords "spotters shells".

Internet safety

When using the Internet, please follow the **Internet safety guidelines** shown on the Usborne Quicklinks Website.

WEBSITE 1 Explore a gallery of seashell pictures and find tips on how to collect and store shells.

WEBSITE 2 Watch videos and see pictures of a variety of cephalopods, such as cuttlefish, octopus and squid.

WEBSITE 3 A useful interactive guide to shell identification.

WEBSITE 4 An illustrated guide to seashells.

WEBSITE 5 Shell activities, games and jokes.

WEBSITE 6 Pictures and movies of some the endangered molluscs featured in this book.

WEBSITE 7 Pictures and lots of useful information about different types of molluscs.

WEBSITE 8 Visit a virtual shell gallery and learn about the different parts of a shell.

WEBSITE 9 Advice on collecting and cleaning shells.

WEBSITE 10 Photos and detailed profiles of a huge variety of shells.

INDEX

63